Parenting Teenagers for Positive Results

VIDEO CURRICULUM PARTICIPANT GUIDE

Jim Burns, Ph.D.

AN INTERACTIVE VIDEO COURSE

FOR SMALL GROUPS AND SUNDAY SCHOOL

 LOVELAND, COLORADO

Group's R.E.A.L. Guarantee to you:

Every Group resource incorporates our R.E.A.L. approach to ministry— a unique philosophy that results in long-term retention and life transformation. It's ministry that's:

This is EARL. He's R.E.A.L. mixed up. (Get it?)

Relational
Because student-to-student interaction enhances learning and builds Christian friendships.

Experiential
Because what students experience sticks with them up to 9 times longer than what they simply hear or read.

Applicable
Because the aim of Christian education is to be both hearers and doers of the Word.

Learner-based
Because students learn more and retain it longer when the process is designed according to how they learn best.

DEDICATION

To Doug and Linda Daniels, Steve and Sue Perry, Craig and Wendy Smith, Bill and Lynda Peters, John and Simone Smernoff, and Steve and Kim Wann. There could not be a more wonderful couples group on the planet Earth. What a joy to raise our families together, to go through good times and hard times together. As someone who came dragging his feet to this group so many years ago, I am grateful for your friendship, love, and encouragement. You were the guinea pigs on this project and you didn't even know it!

PARENTING TEENAGERS FOR POSITIVE RESULTS: VIDEO CURRICULUM KIT
Copyright © 2001 Jim Burns

Visit our Web site: **www.grouppublishing.com**

CREDITS
Author: Jim Burns
Editor: Kelli B. Trujillo
Creative Development Editor: Jim Kochenburger
Chief Creative Officer: Joani Schultz
Copy Editor: Lyndsay E. Bierce
Book Designer: Jean Bruns
Computer Graphic Artist: Tracy K. Donaldson
Cover Art Director/Designer: Jeff A. Storm
Cover Photographer: Blanca Middlebrook
Illustrator: Jim Edmon
Production Manager: Dodie Tipton

Unless otherwise noted, Scripture taken from the HOLY BIBLE, NEW INTERNATIONAL VERSION®. Copyright © 1973, 1978, 1984 by International Bible Society. Used by permission of Zondervan Publishing House. All rights reserved.

LIBRARY OF CONGRESS CATALOGING-IN-PUBLICATION DATA
Burns, Jim, 1953-
    Parenting teenagers for positive results : video curriculum kit / by Jim Burns.
        p. cm.
    "Parenting essentials for strong families."
    Includes bibliographical references.
    ISBN 0-7644-1304-X (alk. paper)
    1. Teenagers--Religious life. 2. Parenting--Religious aspects--Christianity. 3. Family--Religious life. I. Title.

BV4531.2 .B8735 2001
248.8'45--dc21
                                                                2001023816

10 9 8 7 6 5 4 3 2 1   10 09 08 07 06 05 04 03 02 01
Printed in the United States of America.

acknowledgments

Thank you to Cathy for twenty-six years of marriage and for truly being an inspirational parent to our three teenage daughters. Thank you for caring enough to make a difference in their lives. Thank you to Christy, Rebecca, and Heidi for being our "lab."

Thank you to Group Publishing. It is a pleasure to work with such fine people as Thom and Joani Schultz. Thank you for your years of positive influence and impact in the church community worldwide. You are definitely the leader in curriculum publishing in the world today. A special thanks to Jim Kochenburger for your enthusiasm. I caught your vision! Thank you so very much to Kelli Trujillo and Bryan Belknap. You both are an absolute pleasure to work with.

A final word of thanks to a most incredible staff of people at YouthBuilders, who sacrifice so much to influence so many. I love you and consider it a privilege to work alongside you to make a difference in the lives of families, young people, and youth workers. A very special thanks to Carrie Hicks for being a wonderful assistant and much more. Thank you Todd Dean, Kim Dixon, Dean Bruns, Mary Perdue, Rick Olson, Mindy Borg, Mike DeVries, Carrie Johnson, Jim Liebelt, Alison McKay, Bill Reed, Jill Corey, Susie Post, and the hundreds of people who are committed to the YouthBuilders vision. *Thank you.*

Jim Burns, Ph.D.

President, YouthBuilders

San Juan Capistrano, California

www.youthbuilders.com

For more information about YouthBuilders, call 1-800-397-9725

contents

Introduction 5

SESSION ONE
Attitude Is Everything .9

SESSION TWO
Self-Image Struggles .22

SESSION THREE
Communicating With Your Kids 36

SESSION FOUR
Navigating Sexuality .52

SESSION FIVE
Developing Media Discernment 66

SESSION SIX
Helping Your Teenager Grow Spiritually 82

Participant Guide Endnotes 96

introduction

There is a wonderful growing movement in the church toward small groups and cell groups of people getting together around a topic of mutual interest. In the world of youth and family ministry, there has been a crying need for more and better interactive parent workbooks for small group communication. This project comes out of a personal need and a need in the family-based youth ministry community.

Cathy and I have three teenagers. We have never been so humbled and yet honored as we are to raise these three somewhat strong-willed girls in our family. I can't say that we have enjoyed every minute of it, but we sure wouldn't change it. The personal need for this project came from our couples group, who asked me to lead a series on topics for parents and teenagers. Cathy and I found the discussion and sharing of ideas to be an immeasurable help in our own family.

The other reason for writing this material came from a steady cry from youth workers, Sunday school teachers, family ministry people, and parents for more material like this to help parents of teenagers and preteens steer their kids through the unique world of adolescence. Is it more difficult for the teenager or the parent of the teenager? You'll have to decide!

PARENTING TEENAGERS FOR POSITIVE RESULTS

It's Relational—These sessions are geared for interaction. You learn most when you and others discuss a point, instead of just listening to a lecture.

It's Experiential—Studies show that people learn best when they are *involved* in the material. That's why there are case studies, discussion starters, videos, activities, and more.

It's Applicable—The question must always be asked, "Now that I have learned this principle, what am I going to do about it?" Every session has a "So What?" section to help you apply what you've learned to your everyday life.

It's Learner-Based—This was written for my couples group. We needed help with the changes that were taking place in our kids' lives (and our own!). We needed practical answers and easy-to-understand principles. Each session is designed to help meet *your* needs as a participant.

It's Biblical—The Bible may not *look* like a parenting manual, but within its God-breathed pages are the principles needed to raise healthy kids and to run the race with them successfully in a changing and challenging world.

It's Adaptable—You can pick and choose the topics or go straight through the material. You can use this material in a variety of settings, such as:

- Small groups or cell groups
- Individual study and reflection
- Home study between husband and wife
- Adult Sunday school
- Midweek Bible studies
- Retreats and camps
- Special seminars

It's Proven—These sessions were not written by someone in an ivory tower. They were written *by* a parent *for* parents of teenagers and preteens. It has been meaningful in my life and the lives of the families in my small group.

How to Use This Material

Each session is divided into five main parts.

Getting Started

This is the warm-up, where you can forget about the worries of the day and begin to focus on the topic at hand.

Going Deeper

This section takes a deeper look at the topic and is always interactive. Here you'll receive more in-depth information and begin discussing the issues.

In the Word

The Bible contains the answers for excellent Christian parenting skills. Here you'll dig into the Scripture and cover a series of main points that tackle the issues.

So What?

Here you'll be challenged to apply the biblical principles you've discussed. This section contains discussion questions as well as an opportunity for you to commit to one specific action step for the next week.

HomeWork

This is perhaps the most important part of each session. It's a thirty-minute family devotion for you to do at home with your teenager. This is your chance to get together with your child and wrestle with some of the same important principles you discussed in the group.

Video Clips and Bonus Ideas

Keeping Up With the Joneses—Meet Nelson, Carole, Bud, and Susie, characters on the popular TV "classic" *Keeping Up With the Joneses*. In each session you'll have an opportunity to view and discuss a video clip from the Joneses' "idyllic" TV life.

A Word From Jim—Here you'll get a chance to hear from Jim Burns face-to-face in a video clip that highlights the topics of each session.

For Extra Impact—Every session contains an optional For Extra Impact activity or suggestion that can add to your group's exploration of the topic.

Talk About It—These simple suggestions for talking with your teenager can help you build a closer relationship with your son or daughter. Use these ideas at home to prompt meaningful and memorable conversations.

Extra Impact@Home—In addition to the HomeWork family devotion ideas, use these optional activities to explore the issues even more deeply with your teenager.

attitude is everything

Getting Started

Why is it that, somewhere in the early teen years, most kids "cop an attitude"? What happened to that sweet, compliant child who once came running up to you with great enthusiasm and excitement but is now embarrassed to be seen with you in public? Your teenager's favorite phrase is "That's not fair!" and in his or her mind you are the most conservative parent in the entire universe. Many parents experience firsthand the title of a popular book on adolescents, *Get Out of My Life, But First Could You Drive Me and Cheryl to the Mall?*[1]

Nagging doesn't work. Complaining doesn't work. Our own irritable attitudes don't seem to make much of a difference. Shame-based parenting may make a dent for a short time, but it will do damage over the long haul. The 'tudes teenagers develop can often be intense, emotional, and disturbing. As parents, we must realize that our children are going through a unique time of life in which they are moving from dependence to independence. Their emotions are raw, and there is so much being thrown at them that is new and sometimes upsetting. We are called to help our children become responsible adults, and that includes helping them create a healthy, positive attitude and outlook for life.

Take a turn introducing yourself and telling the others a bit about your teenager or preteen by answering one of the following questions:

•What is one special memory you have of your son or daughter as a young child?

• What is one personality trait that you really love about your son or daughter?

Discuss the following question, and then list three "attitude busters."

• What are three things about your life and family that can really bust up your attitude or your teenager's attitude?

_____

_____

_____

Brainstorm and list three "attitude boosters."

• What are three things that can give your attitude and your teenager's attitude the boost you need to have a good day?

_____

_____

_____

_____

Stand up and face your spouse or another parent. One of you will act as the other's mirror. As one partner moves or gestures, the mirror partner should try to replicate the motions exactly. After about one minute, switch roles. Then discuss the following questions:

• What was it like to watch someone mirror all of your actions? How is this similar to your relationship with your teenager?

• In what ways is your child a reflection of you? your good qualities? your shortcomings?

• When have you seen your own attitude reflected in your child's behavior?

Having a positive attitude isn't always easy, even for the Joneses! **Watch the brief video segment,** *and then discuss the following question in your group:*

• *Is your home ever like the Joneses'? How?*

keeping up with the Joneses

Going Deeper

What is always amazing to me is that two children coming from the same home background can be so different when it comes to their attitudes. You are about to meet six teenagers who have some serious work to do on their attitudes. Take some time to read through the attitude case studies, and then discuss the questions that follow.

ATTITUDE CASE STUDIES

Apathetic Andy—Andy seems to have lost all interest in...well, just about *everything*. When his parents try to engage him in conversation, he communicates that he doesn't really care about anything. He sometimes seems so distant—like he's on another planet.

Too-Cool Tara—Tara is just way *too cool* to be seen with Mom and Dad. She makes it clear to her parents that they are definitely out of style and are from the Stone Age. Tara considers herself the only "cool" person in the household.

Moody Mark—Mark's moods are unpredictable. He is happy and content one minute, extremely angry and frustrated the next. Sometimes he even seems fairly depressed. His moods are like a roller coaster—up, down, up, down, and up again. His parents are starting to feel a little dizzy from the ride!

Always-Right Angie—Angie is *always* right. In any conversation (or argument) she will prove her point 'til the very end. She seems to consider herself mentally superior to every other family member. Getting her to sincerely apologize about anything can be like pulling teeth.

Grunts-Only Greg—Greg speaks only in grunts and monosyllables: "Huh?...Yeah...I dunno...Uhhh." His parents are baffled as to how to communicate with him. They just can't seem to get his "language" right. Greg's grunting makes them feel like they aren't important to him. After all, he's not even willing to expend the energy to offer up two (maybe even three!) words in conversation.

Grown-Up Gertrude—Gert seems to have grown up *fast*. At the tender age of thirteen, she already considers herself an adult and cannot understand why her parents don't view her the same way. She cannot *comprehend* how her parents have rules for her regarding curfews, dating, and clothes. After all, she *is* practically old enough to drive with a learner's permit!

1. Which child most closely resembles your child or children? Which of the above identities best describes your own attitude as a teenager? Can you add any attitudes to the list?

2. Which attitude bothers you the most, and why?

3. Which attitude have you battled the most in your home? What types of feelings, struggles, or experiences do you think lead to your teenager's attitudes?

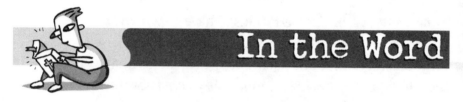

In the Word

Depending on the children's ages and environment, negative attitudes become a major issue in many families. Here's a Bible study on thankfulness that can get you and your family truly thinking on a higher level.

THANKFULNESS TRANSCENDS CIRCUMSTANCES

4. Read 1 Thessalonians 5:16-18. What aspect of this passage is the most challenging to you in your relationship with your teenager?

5. How does the phrase "Thankfulness transcends circumstances" relate to your life? your family members' lives? When have you seen it at work?

6. Read Matthew 6:25-34. How would you summarize the main principles of this passage? How does it challenge you personally?

7. In what types of circumstances in your family life do you find it most difficult to find joy and a positive attitude?

8. How can the advice of Jesus in Matthew 6:34 help you overcome the circumstances that trigger wrong attitudes?

An Attitude Adjustment

Many would say one of the major characteristics of the teenage years is transition. Most people (including us parents) don't do change and transition very well. With all the new things going on in the life and home of a teenager, there is often a greater degree of emotions and attitude issues than in the childhood and preteen years. David Elkind, in his classic book on the adolescent years, *All Grown Up and No Place to Go*[2], calls these years the "unplaced years." Your child is going through major physiological changes. He or she isn't a child anymore and is not yet an adult. That can be pretty tough!

As young people move into this experimental phase of their lives, they may need help with a few attitude adjustments along the way. Attitudes are contagious—consider how your *own* attitude adjustment might affect your family's home life.

a word from **Jim**

Watch this video segment *from Jim Burns, and consider how it applies to your family's life.*

Notes:

9. Practice "thank therapy." Write down ten specific reasons why you are thankful for your family. Share these with your group.

1. _____

2. _____

3. _____

4. _____

5. _____

6. _____

7. _____

8. _____

9. _____

10. _____

10. What's the attitude adjustment found in 1 Thessalonians 5:18?

A THANKFUL ATTITUDE IS GOD'S WILL

11. Read the comments below, and discuss the wisdom behind each statement.

• *Jesus Christ is the ultimate reason for our thankful attitude.*

- *Life's too short to focus on the mundane rather than the miraculous.*

- *Your circumstances may never change, but your attitude can change, and that makes all the difference.*

So What?

12. All three of the points above are true. Which one relates to your family the most, and why?

13. Why is thankfulness such a strong influence on our attitudes? What decisions can you make to help keep your family on a more thankful track?

14. As a group, spend a moment brainstorming several ways to help kids through their struggles with attitudes.

ACTION STEP

• What is one specific step you can take to help your teenager deal with this issue?

TALK About It

The next time your teenager is having a bad day or is in a bad mood, take the time to sincerely and patiently ask how he or she is doing. Your teenager may not feel like talking then...so be patient! You may need to ask when the mood blows over. This is not the time to lecture but to simply listen and not judge.

HomeWork

Set aside thirty minutes this week to do this devotion as a family.

AFFIRMATION BOMBARDMENT

Read Hebrews 10:24-25 together, and discuss the following questions:

• According to this Scripture, what types of positive effects can we have on one another's faith? How can we have these effects?

• Based on your own experiences, what types of negative effects do you think we can have on one another?

• How can our family spur one another on toward love and good deeds? Be specific.

• Name a specific time and situation in the past when you felt affirmed and encouraged by a family member. How did it make you feel?

• What holds us back from an atmosphere of encouragement and affirmation in our home?

Take turns speaking several words of affirmation and encouragement to each family member. To help get the Bombardment started, have each person write down three positive, encouraging words about each family member. Once you've all finished writing, share your affirmations aloud.

Read Psalm 136 together, and then discuss your family's own faith journey.

This psalm roughly follows the progress of events from Creation (Genesis) to the entrance into the Promised Land of Canaan (Joshua). At every step, God demonstrated his love and mercy.

Brainstorm six milestones in the life of your family, and fill in the blanks to form a praise of thanksgiving.

EXAMPLE:

The Lord formed me in my mother's womb.

His love endures forever.

_____

His love endures forever.

_____

His love endures forever.

_____

His love endures forever.

_____

His love endures forever.

_____

His love endures forever.

As a family, take a few moments to pray and thank God for the milestones in one another's lives.

self-image struggles

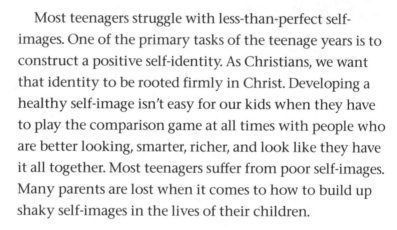

Getting Started

Most teenagers struggle with less-than-perfect self-images. One of the primary tasks of the teenage years is to construct a positive self-identity. As Christians, we want that identity to be rooted firmly in Christ. Developing a healthy self-image isn't easy for our kids when they have to play the comparison game at all times with people who are better looking, smarter, richer, and look like they have it all together. Most teenagers suffer from poor self-images. Many parents are lost when it comes to how to build up shaky self-images in the lives of their children.

Kids struggle in a number of areas when it comes to improper self-images, but many experts tell us that parents can help, especially in the areas of beauty, brains, and bucks. Most adolescents have a strong need for their physical appearance to measure up to the cultural norm. We have to help our kids realize that, even if they don't look like the latest model or sports hero, they will make it in life. Kids tell us that two of the major pressures in their lives are school pressure and the need to please parents. Many kids mention that when it comes to grades, as far as their parents are concerned, "It's never good enough." Money and material wealth are becoming issues of self-image more and more often. Kids must learn that success is not spelled m-o-n-e-y.

We can help build up our teenagers' shaky self-images. But it will take some work on our part. We must help our children remember the difference between how the world views success and how God views success.

What were you like as a teenager? Share your answer to one of the following questions with the group:

• What did you look like as a teenager? How would you describe your "style"?

• What activities were you involved in as a teenager?

• What was your personality like when you were a teenager?

BEAUTY, BRAINS, AND BUCKS

Search through teen magazines to select a picture, advertisement, or article that contributes to negative self-esteem messages for teenagers, and share it with the rest of the group. Then, as a group, create a "Top-Ten" list of incorrect messages the world tells kids about their self-images. For example, some false messages could be "If you have acne, you are ugly" or "If you aren't athletic, you're a nobody."

THE SELF-IMAGE QUESTIONNAIRE

The Bible says we were "created in God's image." Yet most of our children (and most of us!) struggle with an improper or negative view of self. This causes a lack of confidence and, sometimes, destructive behavior patterns. Here's a little questionnaire for you and your child to take a look at self-image. Fill this out, and discuss it with your spouse or one other parent.

1. Is your child a critical person?

2. Is he/she a poor listener?

3. Is he/she argumentative with friends or family?

4. Would you consider your child to be an angry person?

5. Is your child a forgiving person?

6. Is he/she extremely impressed with titles, honors, or degrees?

7. Does your child have difficulty accepting compliments from others?

8. Do the people who know your child consider him/her overly sensitive?

9. Does he/she always have to be right?

10. Is your child a jealous person?

11. Does he/she find it difficult to lose in games and sports or any other events?

• Everyone has traits he or she needs to work on. Using the questionnaire as a guide, list three areas in which your teenager needs the most improvement and three areas in which he or she is doing well.

• What can you do to begin working on his or her more difficult areas?

• How does your self-image as an adult sometimes affect your child's self-image?

keeping up with the Joneses

Even Bud and Susie Jones struggle with self-image issues. **Watch the video segment,** *and then discuss the following questions in your group:*

• *How did you see the drive for beauty, brains, or bucks illustrated in this segment?*

• *How do you see these things in* your *home?*

Going Deeper

BUILDING UP A SHAKY SELF-IMAGE

Building positive, healthy, Christ-centered self-images in our children is one of the primary tasks of all parents.

Frankly, I have seldom, if ever, seen a child who is involved in drug abuse, suicide attempts, or other patterns of self-destructive behavior have a healthy self-image. The diagrams on pages 27 and 28 illustrate the negative cycles that young people can find themselves in when dealing with their own self-images.

Watch this video segment *from Jim Burns, and consider how it applies to your family's life.*

a word from Jim

Notes:

As a group, look at the negative self-image cycle and the inferiority cycle, and then discuss the questions that follow.

The Negative Self-Image Cycle

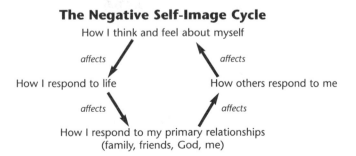

How I think and feel about myself

affects

affects

How I respond to life

How others respond to me

affects

affects

How I respond to my primary relationships
(family, friends, God, me)

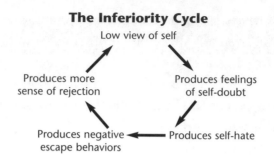

The Inferiority Cycle

Low view of self

Produces more sense of rejection

Produces feelings of self-doubt

Produces negative escape behaviors

Produces self-hate

1. How do these cycles affect your teenager and your family?

2. What do you see as possible negative escape behaviors in teenagers? Do you see any negative escape behaviors in your own child?

3. What can you do to help stop this negative self-image cycle from getting worse in your teenager's life?

In the Word

This section consists of four practical steps to helping you develop a proper self-image in your child. As you look at each of these points and discuss the questions, think of how you can provide ways to instill these principles into the life of your child.

HELP YOUR TEENAGERS VIEW THEMSELVES AS GOD DOES

4. Read Ephesians 2:10. How does God view you and your child?

5. What makes his love for you and your teenager so special?

6. How can you bring this truth home to your teenager more effectively?

Accept God's Forgiveness

7. Read 1 John 1:9 and Isaiah 43:25. What does God promise to do in these verses?

• *How can embracing God's forgiveness affect one's self-image?*

• *How can* not *embracing God's forgiveness affect one's self-image?*

8. Because God's ways are different than our ways, it is sometimes difficult to accept God's forgiveness. It is also hard to forgive ourselves, even after God has forgiven us. What are a few areas in your life in which you have confessed your sin to God, yet still have trouble forgiving yourself? What are forgiveness issues your child may be struggling with in his or her life?

9. Do you believe your child understands the biblical concept of forgiveness? What can you do to help him or her know and feel forgiveness from God?

Become Others-Centered

10. Read Matthew 16:24-25 and Philippians 2:3-4. How can focusing on the needs of others instead of focusing on ourselves affect the way we feel about ourselves? How can you instill this trait in your child?

11. What are some specific things you can do within the next month to be a more others-centered person? What can you do together as a family to be more others-centered?

Here are a few ideas to become a more others-centered person:

- do favors for friends or family,
- give compliments, and
- be an available listener.

Stay Healthy

An important factor in a proper self-image is taking care of your body. It is very important to watch what you eat, keep your body in good physical shape, get plenty of sleep, and have enough time for relaxation.

12. Read 1 Corinthians 6:19-20. Take a moment to fill out the chart below on your own. How are you doing in each of these areas? How is your child doing?

You	Your Children
Eating Habits:	Eating Habits:
Staying Physically Fit:	Staying Physically Fit:
Sleep:	Sleep:
Relaxation:	Relaxation:

If any of these areas need work, write down a few specific goals to work on in the coming weeks.

You	Your Children
Staying Physically Fit *Goal: Walk four times this week for 30 minutes with my spouse.*	Sleep *Goal: Hold my child accountable to eight plus hours of sleep per night.*

So What?

13. How do you think your own self-image struggles affect your teenager? What can you do to improve your own self-image?

ACTION STEP

• What is one specific step you can take to help build up your teenager's self-image?

TALK About It

Share with your teenager how you struggled with your self-image as a teenager and perhaps even as an adult. Be honest and vulnerable.

Set aside thirty minutes this week to do this devotion as a family. Read these case studies, and then discuss the questions below.

CASE STUDIES

Janet

Janet often played the very dangerous comparison game in her mind. She always lost. She compared her looks to others, and there was always someone who was prettier. She compared her athletic ability, money, and even her school grades, and in her mind she always came up a loser.

- What advice would you give Janet?

- Do you know anyone like Janet? What is he or she like?

Terry

Terry was very upset with his parents because "everybody else wore" really expensive brand-name tennis shoes, and his parents refused to buy him a pair. Terry wanted his physical appearance to measure up to the cultural norm, and his parents wouldn't let him wear the right tennis shoes or get his hair cut the way some of his friends wore their hair.

- What advice would you give this family?

- Do you know anyone like Terry? What is he or she like?

• Read 1 Samuel 16:4-13. How was Samuel's perspective of Eliab similar to the way we often view others?

• According to the first part of verse 7, what was Samuel focused on? What types of superficial things do we often focus on when we view others? when we view ourselves?

• How was God's perspective of what is important different than Samuel's?

• What does 1 Samuel 16:7 mean in our own lives? How will it affect the way we view ourselves?

Conclude the family devotion by verbally sharing an affirmation with your teenager, telling him or her something about his or her character—what's in his or her heart—that you value and appreciate.

Extra Impact @ HOME

God's values are different from those of the world. At home with your teenager, take a piece of paper and write on one side the words, "The World's Values" and on the other side, "God's Values." Brainstorm together a list of values for each side, and discuss how these values can affect one's self-image.

Then have family members write on pieces of paper ten reasons why they should like themselves. Encourage family members to put their lists in places where they'll see them throughout the week. Put the "God's Values" list on the refrigerator as a reminder to focus on what God thinks is important.

communicating with your kids

Getting Started

Keeping the communication lines open is a must with our children. But what can we do to keep their spirits open, even in the midst of inevitable conflict? If you are having an easy time communicating with your teenager, you are among the small minority of parents. You may have noticed that something quite strange happens to many kids as they enter adolescence. Communication used to be pretty easy—your small child would sit on your lap after school, laughing and telling you all about his or her day. Now your child slinks past you to his or her room, slams and locks the door, turns on the music so loud that your windows shake, and talks on the phone for hours...but only speaks to you in grunts unless he or she wants money.

Despite the fact that parents and teenagers seem to communicate on very different levels, it is a must that both teenagers and parents work on making the communication thing happen. Communicating with someone on the same planet is challenging enough, but when you seem to come from two very different worlds, it makes communication downright difficult. But as you well know, there are moments, glimpses if you will, when you see that quality communication is possible. It just takes a lot of work.

Share with the group your answer to one of the following questions:

• What's a funny miscommunication you've had with someone in your family? Or what's a memorable example of miscommunication you've seen on TV?

• What is one difference between you and your teenager that's surprising or funny?

COMMUNICATION BARRIERS

Stand up with a partner, and begin telling him or her about your day. Listen for the leader's instructions as you physically experience various communication challenges. When you've finished, sit back down and discuss the following questions with your group:

• What was challenging or difficult about trying to communicate without being face-to-face? How did the challenges increase as you stepped farther away from your partner?

• How is this activity similar to the communication barriers you face with your teenager? What are some of those barriers?

THE COMMUNICATION QUESTIONNAIRE

Answer these questions with members of your group:

1. How was the communication with your parents when you were a teenager? What do you wish your parents had done differently?

2. On a scale of 1 to 10, how would you say communication is going with your teenager?

1	2	3	4	5	6	7	8	9	10

We barely speak   It's just OK   We can talk
to each other   about anything

Emergency room   **We could use**   **So far**
needed   **some help**   **so good**

(more →)

3. What is the number-one cause of conflict or mis-communication with your teenager?

4. What do you wish would take place in the communication with your teenager? What could you do differently?

For EXTRA Impact

Think of a recent conflict you had with your teenager. What details do you recall? Share a play-by-play of the conflict with another parent, and then ask for his or her honest feedback about how you could have handled the situation differently.

Nobody is perfect—not even the Joneses! **Watch the video segment,** *and then discuss the following questions in your group:*

* *What are your expectations of communication with your teenager? Are they realistic? unrealistic?*

keeping
up
with
the
Joneses

Conflict in the home is almost always inevitable. Conflict with teenagers is a norm. Take a moment to read through the "Paths of Conflict" diagram on pages 42 and 43 and to discuss it with your group.

We all struggle with taking the high road when it comes to dealing with conflict. Because of our family backgrounds or past painful experiences, we tend to deal with conflict by being defensive and closed with an intent to protect ourselves, as opposed to the sometimes more difficult but high path, which is being open and nondefensive with an intent to learn and to assume responsibility.

1. Look at the diagram and review the left-hand side. When you are operating with the intent to protect, are you

- *more permissive or authoritarian?*

- *controlling, compliant, or indifferent?*

2. What areas of the "intent to learn" side of the diagram do you want to work on?

3. What areas of this entire diagram does your child need to work on? How would it be helpful to go through the diagram with your child?

In the Word

COMMUNICATION: JESUS STYLE

Jesus was the "master communicator" throughout the gospels. He dealt with everything from conflict to love with integrity and honesty. Our job as parents is to learn to be the most effective communicators we can possibly be, understanding that we can learn a great deal from the way Jesus handled people.

4. Read Mark 10:13-16, and list ways Jesus communicated to

- *the children,*

- *the parents,*

- *his disciples.*

The Path of Unloving Behavior
(Ego)

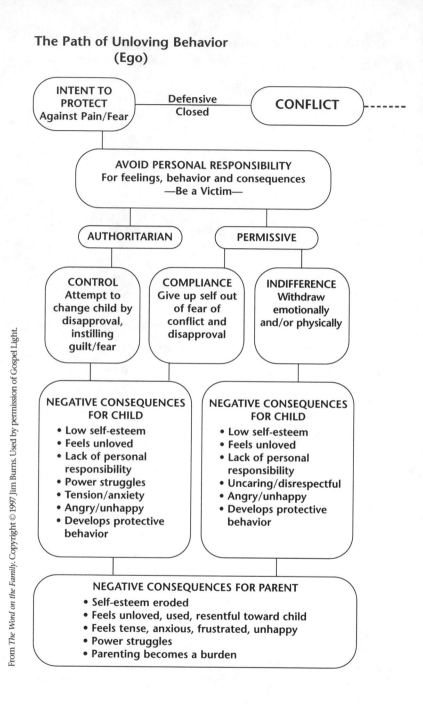

INTENT TO PROTECT
Against Pain/Fear

Defensive
Closed

CONFLICT

- - - - - -

AVOID PERSONAL RESPONSIBILITY
For feelings, behavior and consequences
—Be a Victim—

AUTHORITARIAN

PERMISSIVE

CONTROL
Attempt to change child by disapproval, instilling guilt/fear

COMPLIANCE
Give up self out of fear of conflict and disapproval

INDIFFERENCE
Withdraw emotionally and/or physically

NEGATIVE CONSEQUENCES FOR CHILD
- Low self-esteem
- Feels unloved
- Lack of personal responsibility
- Power struggles
- Tension/anxiety
- Angry/unhappy
- Develops protective behavior

NEGATIVE CONSEQUENCES FOR CHILD
- Low self-esteem
- Feels unloved
- Lack of personal responsibility
- Uncaring/disrespectful
- Angry/unhappy
- Develops protective behavior

NEGATIVE CONSEQUENCES FOR PARENT
- Self-esteem eroded
- Feels unloved, used, resentful toward child
- Feels tense, anxious, frustrated, unhappy
- Power struggles
- Parenting becomes a burden

From *The Word on the Family*. Copyright © 1997 Jim Burns. Used by permission of Gospel Light.

The Path of Loving Behavior
(Higher Self)

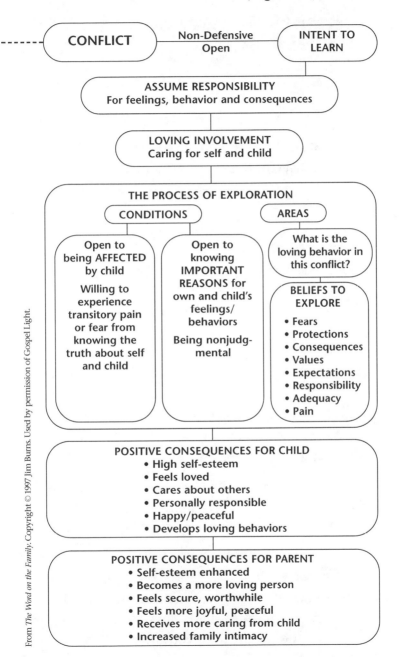

CONFLICT — Non-Defensive Open — INTENT TO LEARN

ASSUME RESPONSIBILITY
For feelings, behavior and consequences

LOVING INVOLVEMENT
Caring for self and child

THE PROCESS OF EXPLORATION

CONDITIONS

Open to being AFFECTED by child

Willing to experience transitory pain or fear from knowing the truth about self and child

Open to knowing IMPORTANT REASONS for own and child's feelings/ behaviors

Being nonjudgmental

AREAS

What is the loving behavior in this conflict?

BELIEFS TO EXPLORE

• Fears
• Protections
• Consequences
• Values
• Expectations
• Responsibility
• Adequacy
• Pain

POSITIVE CONSEQUENCES FOR CHILD
• High self-esteem
• Feels loved
• Cares about others
• Personally responsible
• Happy/peaceful
• Develops loving behaviors

POSITIVE CONSEQUENCES FOR PARENT
• Self-esteem enhanced
• Becomes a more loving person
• Feels secure, worthwhile
• Feels more joyful, peaceful
• Receives more caring from child
• Increased family intimacy

THE POWER OF BEING THERE

5. Reread Mark 10:13-14. Why do you think the disciples rebuked the parents?

6. What was Jesus' response to the disciples rebuking the parents? What emotions do you think he displayed?

7. How did Jesus show his availability to the children?

Being available—being there—can have a powerful effect on our kids. Your child regards your very presence in his or her life as a sign of caring and connectedness. Some parents are too busy and overcommitted, while other parents are available and practice the power of being there.

Many teenagers do not believe their parents are available to them, and yet most parents say they are absolutely available. What do you think your child would say?

Often, studies on the priorities of teenagers will baffle parents because they show that a vast majority of kids do desire a relationship with their parents and actually do want them very much in their lives. Believe it or not, your teenager may act like he or she doesn't want you around...but he or she really does! (Just not out in front of the school, mall, movie theater, or other teen hangouts. That is *unless* you are paying and it is not a Friday or Saturday night.)

8. What aspects of your life compete for your time with your child?

9. How do you offer your availability to your child? How is it received?

THE POWER OF AFFECTION

Just as Jesus illustrates in Mark 10:16, touch and affection are true forms of offering a blessing. Obviously, most high school or junior high students do not want their parents to hug and kiss them out in front of the school. However, there *is* a deep need for appropriate touch and affection from family.

Read this case study, and discuss the questions that follow.

Karen is sixteen years old. She loves her dad and mom, but no one in the family really expresses love much through words or with hugs. Her mom feeds her and takes care of her as an expression of love, and her dad provides for her needs by making a good living and working long hours. Karen started dating a boy who was a few years older. They quickly became very sexually involved. When she told her youth leader about the relationship, she said, "I didn't want to go so far sexually, but I just feel so special when Brandon tells me he loves me and holds me."

10. How did Karen's unmet need for affection from her parents affect her decisions? What advice would you give Karen or her parents?

11. How would you rate the physical affection comfort level in your home?

1	2	3	4	5	6	7	8	9	10

Cold as ice   Occasional   Tons of hugs

handshakes

If you are not a person who communicates your love for your child through appropriate physical affection, then it is not too late to start. This week, communicate with your teenager through words of affection and an appropriate hug. Find natural ways to express your affection daily.

Just in case there has been little or no physical affection in the home, your child might really think you are weird if you suddenly start hugging your child and telling him or her you love him or her. Here are a few ideas for you:

- Play a game together.
- Give an affectionate touch on the arm.
- Sustain eye contact.
- Sit with an inviting posture when your child interrupts you.
- Write a note to tell your child how proud you are of him or her.
- Affirm your child in front of a family friend or relative.
- Wrestle with your child.
- Bring home a gift.

Can you think of other ways?

THE POWER OF WORDS

Meaningful touch may even be more powerful than words, but without the right words, the blessing cannot be completed. There is great power in words, both positive words and negative ones. Positive words bless and build up, while negative words tear apart and curse.

12. Share with your group some words that have affected you in your lifetime.

> • *Share a positive word, statement, or phrase. Who said it, and what did that person say? How have these words affected you?*

> • *Share a negative word, statement, or phrase. Who said it, and what did that person say? How have these words affected you?*

So What?

13. In Mark 10:16, imagine for a moment that Jesus was speaking to your child. What words of blessing would he offer your child?

14. How can you communicate this same blessing to your child?

15. What areas of communication—Jesus style—are you most effective in with your child? (Circle one.) Which one could use some improvement? (Underline one.)

- *The Power of Being There*
- *The Power of Affection*
- *The Power of Words*

ACTION STEP

- What is one specific step you can take to improve the communication between you and your teenager?

TALK About It

Ask your teenager how he or she would like the communication to improve between the two of you. What frustrates him or her? Don't defend yourself...just listen.

HomeWork

Set aside thirty minutes this week to do this devotion as a family.

Play a game of Pictionary as a family. If you don't have the board game, simply write a variety of words on several slips of paper. Take turns silently drawing images and symbols, while the rest of the family tries to guess the word you're representing. After the game, discuss the following questions:

• What was the most challenging part about not being able to verbally communicate?

• How are these challenges similar to the challenges we face in everyday communication with one another?

As a family, create a list of the essentials for good communication.

• Read Ephesians 4:29-32 together. What principles of excellent communication are described in these verses? Add these reasons to your list of communication essentials.

• Review the list you've created, and circle the top two areas your family is good at and at least two areas your family wants to work on.

• What is one specific way you'd like communication patterns to improve in your family? What is one specific way your own communication with family members needs to improve?

Take some time to pray together as a family, and don't forget to communicate your needs.

Here are eighteen great phrases to enhance communication. Have each family member choose five phrases they would like to say. Have each person tell the other family members one phrase he or she has chosen and why. After everyone has shared one phrase, have them share the second phrase they have chosen.

I love you.	I care about you.
I need you.	You are special.
What do you think?	How do you feel about it?
What would you do?	I've got a problem.
I need your help.	I blew it.
I made a mistake.	I'm sorry.
I want you to forgive me.	I want to make things better.
You were right.	I was wrong.
Maybe we could just start over.	I shouldn't have said that.

From *The Word on the Family.* Copyright © 1997 Jim Burns.
Used by permission of Gospel Light.

navigating sexuality

Getting Started

Our sexuality is a God-given part of our lives. Unfortunately, children and youth receive far too many messages from the world portraying an unhealthy and ungodly view of sex. Kids today definitely have lots of questions about this subject, and parents can often feel paralyzed when it comes to knowing how to communicate with their kids about this important but delicate subject.

Sometimes parents give too little information, and sometimes they give too much. Here's an example: A seven-year-old boy approached his mother after school one day and casually asked the dreaded question, "Hey, Mom, what is sex?" His mother couldn't believe she was hearing those words; after all, he was only seven years old! And furthermore, where was his father at a time like this? She and her husband had actually talked about the time when their son would be a teenager and they would have the "birds and bees" discussion.

She placed a plate of cookies in front of her seven-year-old and filled his glass with milk. She then began to answer his question with honesty and thoroughness, still wishing her husband were home to help with this delicate teaching. She drew diagrams and didn't leave anything out. Her little son's eyes were as large as saucers, and he just kept eating the cookies. Finally after forty-five minutes, the mother asked, "Son, do you have any more questions?" Her son replied, "Yeah, Mom, just one." As he showed her his soccer application, he continued, "How am I supposed to put all that where it says, 'Sex: male or female' on this application?"

All he really wanted to know was the meaning of the word for his soccer application so he could circle the correct answer. Her "sermonette on sex" was neither asked for nor age appropriate! Unfortunately, the opposite of this story is even more the norm today. The average young person today does not receive much sex education from his or her parents. Only a small number of today's young people say they received positive healthy value-centered information about sexuality from home.

Think back to when you were a teenager, and share your answer to one of these questions with the group:

• When you were a teenager, what was your idea of an "ideal romantic relationship"?

• What impression of married love (and the "birds and the bees") did you get from your parents' relationship?

KIDS MAKING SEXUAL DECISIONS

Kids are making sexual decisions today based on these three reasons:

1. Peer pressure (or the pressure to conform to the cultural norm),
2. Emotional involvement that exceeds their maturity level, and
3. Lack of positive, healthy, value-centered sex education from home and church.

• Can you add any reasons to this list?

• Discuss and write down your thoughts on these three reasons and any others you came up with. What are the problems? What are some of the solutions?

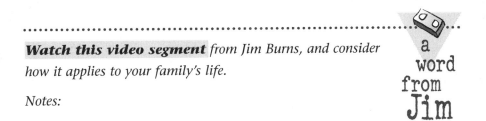

Uh-oh...It looks like it's time for Nelson and Carole to have "the talk" with Bud and Susie. **Watch the video segment,** *and discuss the following question in your group:*

• *Can you relate to any parts of this segment? How?*

keeping up with the Joneses

Watch this video segment *from Jim Burns, and consider how it applies to your family's life.*

Notes:

a word from Jim

KIDS RECEIVE MIXED MESSAGES

When it comes to messages about sexuality, kids receive mixed messages:

At Home—Most young people do not receive much information from their parents.

At Church—Many young people believe the church only presents an old-fashioned or too conservative message about sex. Many churches choose to basically ignore the subject in their curriculum.

In the Media—Music, movies, and television are pleased to present a very liberal view of sexuality. This is the number-one way many young people learn about sex.

• What mixed messages did you receive as a young person?

• What are the mixed messages your children are receiving?

• What can you do to demystify these mixed messages for your children?

For EXTRA Impact

Have an extended prayer time in pairs with your spouse or another parent. Pray for protection and wisdom for your child in the area of sexuality. Pray for the courage to address these issues in the right way with your teenager.

Going Deeper

One common factor that most children and adolescents share is that they have questions about their sexuality. The questions are often simple and innocent, but other times they are frightening for parents. By the time kids are adolescents, their questions are much less about the biological issues and much more about the practical issues. Over the years, YouthBuilders (formerly the National Institute of Youth Ministry) has collected thousands of questions from teenagers who are very vulnerable and honest with their questions. Here is a compiled list of some of the very common and real questions we've received from Christian young people about sex. Read and discuss the list of questions with your spouse or one other parent.

COMMON TEEN QUESTIONS ABOUT SEXUALITY

- How far is too far?

- Is it possible to get the pill without your parents knowing?

- How often do married people usually have sexual intercourse?

- Is oral sex OK?

- How do girls masturbate?

- How do boys masturbate?

- At what age do boys have their first erection?

- When is a girl's most dangerous time of the month? Is the pill expensive? Is the pill dangerous?

• What types of VD are there?

• I'm afraid of AIDS. What can I do to not get it?

• If you participate in oral sex, are you still a virgin?

• Will God condemn you if you have premarital sex? Or will he forgive you?

• What can a guy do if he has a problem of lust toward other guys? How can he handle it without having to be gay?

• Does God forgive Christians who have had abortions?

• After someone has been sexually abused for about five years and hasn't told anyone about it, how can that person try to forget and deal with it?

1. How do these questions make you feel?

2. What are the questions that surprise you?

• challenge you?

• make you mad?

These questions reflect some of the topics on the minds of young people when it comes to sex. As parents, we must not shy away from having meaningful conversations with our children about these very important issues. Now, don't sit down with your teenager (like one mother I know) and go over all of these questions at once! Make a list of the subjects you would like to talk about during this season of your child's life. Look for natural ways to talk with him or her through conversation, tapes, books, videos, or any way you decide to help your child receive good, healthy, positive, value-centered sex education from home. Remember that by far the most effective sex education comes from home. It won't be easy, and you may feel awkward (your child will, too). However, if you don't talk to him or her about these issues, who will?

In the Word

What does the Bible say about sexuality? A lot. One of the key ingredients necessary in positive, value-centered sex education is Scripture. The Bible is quite clear that God is the Creator and Lord of our sexuality.

GOD CREATED OUR SEXUALITY

3. Read Genesis 1:26-31. Describe the role sexuality plays in this passage. How did God describe his creation?

A Healthy Perspective on Sex

4. Read Exodus 20:14. What is the purpose of this commandment? What does it communicate about God's perspective on sex?

5. Read Matthew 19:4-6. What does it mean to be "one flesh"? How can you communicate this concept to your teenager?

God Wants the Best for Us

6. Read 1 Thessalonians 4:3-5. How would you define sexual immorality? What are some of the consequences of sexual immorality?

7. What types of situations can lead to sexual immorality? What types of temptations do teenagers face?

8. Read Philippians 4:8-9. How can this principle help someone deal with sexual temptation? What is God's promise in this passage?

So What?

9. How would you rate your communication with your teenager regarding sexuality?

1	2	3	4	5
Not so hot		Doing OK		Great communication

10. What are the fears or challenges you face when you consider discussing these issues with your teenager?

11. What do you think are the most effective ways you can teach your child these principles?

12. As a group, discuss the ideas and strategies for approaching this topic with your children.

ACTION STEP

• What is one specific action step you can take to help your teenager deal with sexuality issues?

TALK About It

Ask your child how kids at school or in the the teenage culture view sex. Then just listen. This will help you gain a perspective on the pressure your teenager faces.

HomeWork

Set aside thirty minutes this week to do this family devotion.

This can be a very powerful time together with your child. You can either go through this one-on-one with the same-sex parent and child or as a couple with your child.

God's Blueprint for Sex

Attempt to put a puzzle together without using the picture on the top of the box. After five minutes or so of trying, start using the picture on the box top for reference. As you work on the puzzle, intro the topic by getting your child's perspective on how other teenagers and the media view sex. Then discuss the following questions:

• How was putting the puzzle together without the picture to help similar to how our culture approaches sexuality?

• How did using the picture as our guide help us with the project?

• How can God's "blueprint" for sexuality help our culture?

• Read 1 Corinthians 6:18-20. What are the main points of this passage?

• How can making a wise decision on who we date relate to overcoming sexual temptation?

• True or false: Who you date and what you do on your dates will be a decisive factor in how you carry out your Christian commitment. Why did you answer as you did?

• Together brainstorm at least five ways to deal with sexual temptations.

Extra Impact @ HOME

Here are several ideas and resources that can help you talk with your child about sex, dating, and relationships:

- Take your child on an overnighter, and read through a book together.
- Work through a book or curriculum on the subject on a weekly basis.
- Listen to a tape or watch a video together.
- Give your child a purity ring, and discuss the value of saving sex for marriage.
- Encourage your child to sign a sexual purity pledge card.

RESOURCES:

• *Surviving Adolescence*—a book for students and their parents by Jim Burns on the important issues of adolescence, including sex, dating, drugs and alcohol, friendship, and self-image (Gospel Light, 1997).

• *The Word on Sex, Drugs and Rock 'N' Roll*—curriculum for students by Jim Burns on these important issues primarily used for youth ministry but often used with parents and children as well (Gospel Light, 1994).

• *Preparing for Adolescence* book & audio—Dr. James Dobson's "classic" series mainly geared for preteens (book: Regal Books, 1999; audio: Regal Books, 1992).

• Check out the parents' resource section at www.youthbuilders.com for even more resource ideas!

Your church may be involved with the True Love Waits campaign or one of the many outstanding sexual purity programs available. If it isn't, ask your youth worker for more information. You can reproduce the "card" on the next page or create your own. Many young people tell us that they wish their parents had talked more with them about sexuality; few ever wish their parents had remained silent.

The Sexual Purity Pledge

"Do you not know that your bodies are members of Christ himself? ...therefore honor God with your body."

1 Corinthians 6:15, 20

Believing that God's desire for my life and the lives of others is to keep my life sexually pure and refrain from sexual intercourse until the day I enter marriage, I commit my body to God, my future mate, and my family.

_____   _____
SIGNATURE   DATE

developing media discernment

Getting Started

The year was 1964. Ed Sullivan was a household name, and the world watched his Sunday evening variety show on television. I remember hearing Ed Sullivan introduce the Beatles by saying, "Here are the boys from England. Please welcome the Beatles." It looked like every girl in the audience was screaming and crying with excitement. My dad complained about the Beatles' loud music, their hair, and their "silly looking suits and ties." Oh, to bring back the days of Ed Sullivan and the Beatles!

Today's young people watch MTV an average of ten hours a week.[1] Their movies are more sexually explicit than Playboy was in 1964. Full frontal nudity and the F-word are almost the norm on late night cable shows. Life has definitely changed since we were teenagers, and perhaps the greatest shift has been in the area of media.

As parents, we must continue to be students of the culture. Sure, we can complain about the negative influence of much of the media today, but we also must take a proactive approach to teaching our children to discern how to navigate the incredible influence of the media and culture in their lives.

Share your answer to one of the following questions with the group:

• What is your favorite movie, TV show, or song?

• What was your favorite movie, TV show, or song when you were a teenager?

TV Classics Quiz

Test your TV knowledge by trying to fill out this quiz. Once you've finished, share your answers with the group.

1. Can you name all six of the kids from *The Brady Bunch*?

2. Can you name the six main characters from NBC's *Friends*?

3. True or false: MTV's *The Real World* is a heavy-metal music video show.

4. What was Andy Taylor's job on *The Andy Griffith Show*?

5. How many acts of violence will an average elementary school student see on TV from kindergarten through sixth grade?[2]

6. True or false: The average young person has regular opportunities to view sexual innuendo and sexual acts on prime time television.

JUST THE FACTS

Read these media facts as a group.

• *Fact One:* A young person today will spend more hours watching television in a year than being in school.[3]

• *Fact Two:* By the time a child finishes elementary school, he or she will have seen 8,000 televised murders and 100,000 televised acts of violence. By the time the child reaches age eighteen, those numbers will be doubled.[4]

• *Fact Three:* The average young person has the opportunity to view 14,000 simulated acts of intercourse or innuendo to intercourse on prime time television in just one year.[5]

• *Fact Four:* Drug and alcohol use and abuse are a common theme in television, movies, and music with little or no consequences for intoxication. Often drugs and alcohol are glamorized among rock and movie heroes.

THAT WAS THEN AND THIS IS NOW

How do you feel about the above facts? Discuss the following questions in your group:

• Do you think these facts are realistic or alarmist? How often have you observed some of these negative things on TV?

• How have television and other forms of media changed since you were a teenager?

• What is your child's favorite television show?

• How is our culture today different than it was when you were a teenager? Consider these specific areas:

   • *Music*

   • *Movies*

   • *Television*

   • *Internet*

It looks like Susie has been watching some violent stuff! **Watch this brief video segment,** *and then discuss the following question in your group:*

• *Susie's reaction to violence on TV is obviously extreme. How have you seen the effects of popular media in your teenager's life? in your own life?*

Going Deeper

WHAT YOU NEED TO KNOW ABOUT TELEVISION VIOLENCE

Many parents are concerned about the amount of sex and drugs in the media, but we must also be concerned about violence.

The most extensive study on television violence is the National Television Violence Study. Here is a summary of the recent study's key findings:

• Most television violence goes unpunished. In fact, perpetrators go unpunished in 73% of all violent scenes.

• 47% of all violent interactions show no harm to victims.

- 58% of all violent interactions show no pain.
- Only 16% of all violent interactions portray the long-term negative effects of violence (psychological, financial, or emotional harm).
- 25% of all violent interactions involve handguns.
- Only 4% of all violent programs emphasize an anti-violence theme.
- 57% of all programming is violent.

While life can be violent and ugly at times, TV paints an unrealistic picture of what violence is actually like. As a result, kids grow up with a false notion of reality.[6]

FIVE EFFECTS OF TV VIOLENCE

1. Television may lead our children and teens to become immune to the horrors of violence.

2. Children and teens can come to accept violence as a way to solve problems.

3. TV violence serves to make kids more aggressive.

4. Kids might begin to imitate some of the more violent behaviors they have seen on the small screen.

5. Kids develop an unrealistic view of the world.[7]

- Can you add any effects to this list?

• Which of these effects concerns you the most when you think about your own teenager?

What can a parent do? Here are some practical suggestions to help you control and shape your child's viewing habits. With your group, brainstorm at least three more ideas to add to this list.

• Ban programs that are violent or offensive. This requires parental awareness. Watch an episode or two of the show in question. That way, you'll be able to make an informed decision.

• Limit your child's viewing time, and restrict viewing to shows that are educational in nature or shows that demonstrate respect, caring, and concern.

• Process viewing of violent incidents by discussing them with your child. Always discuss the reasons and consequences of the violent incident. Teach your child about right and wrong by sharing your biblically informed analysis.

• Discuss nonviolent responses and biblical solutions to the problems television portrays. Be sure you teach your child that violence is not an acceptable, quick, and easy solution to problems.

• Offer an active alternative to passive television viewing. Get out and play with your teenager. Spend large quantities of quality time talking, working on a hobby, and so on. When kids enjoy good family time, they don't miss TV time!

In the Word

GARBAGE IN, GARBAGE OUT

Several times in the Bible, we learn that what we feed our minds can lead to either problems or joy in our lives.

1. Read the following verses, and create a one-sentence summary of the main principle of each verse.

• *Colossians 3:1-3*

_____

_____

• *Philippians 4:8-9*

_____

_____

• *Isaiah 26:3*

_____

_____

2. Which of these verses strikes you the most? Why?

3. How do these verses relate to the influence of the media in your teenager's life? in your life?

EQUIPPING YOUR TEENAGER TO SET HIGH STANDARDS

Many parents have said that it is very helpful to have clearly established standards for viewing media for their children and the entire family. Most often our children need to understand why our approach may be different than that of the world around them. Romans 12:1-3 is an excellent example of why Christians set high standards. However, by far the most effective way to teach these principles is when we, as parents, model the kind of behavior we wish for our children. Even if, for a time, the kids push the envelope, they will often return to the values of their families as they mature.

a word from Jim

Watch this video segment from Jim Burns, and consider how it applies to your family's life.

Notes:

4. How would you rate your family's viewing standards for TV and movies? (Circle one.)

- Needs a plan.

- It's a struggle.

- We have set high standards, and we are trying to follow them.

5. Read Romans 12:1-3. What do you think Paul meant by "the renewing of your mind" in verse 2? Practically speaking, how can this be accomplished?

6. How can we help our children to renew their minds when it comes to the media?

7. Has your teenager exhibited some of his or her own standards in media choices? Or does he or she rely solely on the standards you've established? How can you help your teenager set some of his or her own high standards?

Using the Media for Positive Results

8. Can you think of any positive ways for the media to influence our children? How can you use the media as a teaching tool?

9. Share with the group a positive media experience or habit you have had with your child.

Although it is not always easy, media can help you connect with your teenager. How about at least one weekly family television hour in which you watch a positive show? Bring out the popcorn and make it an event. Take in a movie or video together. After you have watched the show, take a few minutes to discuss the program without sounding too "preachy" or making it seem like school. Look for opportunities for "hidden curriculum" experiences, even from a negative media exposure. (Our family watches *Touched By an Angel* on a regular basis. Necessary ingredients: popcorn, soft drinks, and tissue for Dad.)

Watch a thought-provoking movie clip or a clip from a prime time television show, and use it as a springboard for discussion. This is great practice for using media as a positive influence in your teenager's life. For movie clip ideas, check out "Mind Over Media" at www.youthministry.com. (In general, federal copyright laws do not allow you to use videos (even ones you own) for any purpose other than home viewing. Though some exceptions allow for the use of short segments of copyrighted material for educational purposes, it's best to be on the safe side. Your church can obtain a license from the Motion Picture Licensing Corporation for a small fee. Just visit www.mplc.com or call 1-800-462-8855 for more information.)

So What?

10. How do these scriptural principles challenge you as your family deals with today's media?

11. What specific concerns do you have regarding media in your teenager's life? What do you think is the best way to approach this issue?

Action Step

• What is one specific step you can take to help your teenager develop media discernment?

TALK About It

Ask your teenager about his or her favorite TV show or music group. Watch it or listen to it. Don't judge or criticize, just try to understand *why* your teenager likes it. This will open the door for future conversations.

HomeWork

Set aside thirty minutes this week to do this devotion as a family.

As a family, brainstorm about several movies, TV shows, or music groups, and decide together where to list them on the various places on the content thermometer—good, neutral, or bad.

• Based on the movies, music, and TV shows you listed by the thermometer, how would you describe the filters you use to decide what to watch and listen to?

• Read together Philippians 4:8. Practically speaking, how does Paul's advice relate to decisions we make about media influence in our lives?

• What are some examples of things to watch, listen to, or think about that meet the standards in Philippians 4:8?

• Compare the Scripture "filter" to the thermometer. Would you move any of the shows, movies, or songs to another category based on Philippians 4:8?

• How do we rate our family's media habits? (Discuss and circle one.)

• *Takin' it all in.*

• *Just the right rules.*

• *Totally too strict.*

Work together to create a family media-viewing contract. Be willing to listen and compromise! Here's a sample to help you get started.

THE MEDIA CONTRACT

1. The average number of hours the TV should be on in our home per day is...

2. The TV programs that are not acceptable in our home are...

3. The movie ratings or movie content that is acceptable for each family member to view are...

4. The family agreement about MTV is...

5. The type of music and radio stations to be listened to by our family includes...

6. The types of books and magazines to be read in our home are...

7. Here is how we will discuss and negotiate differences in opinion...

helping your teenager grow spiritually

Getting Started

One of your primary God-given tasks as a parent is to pass on a spiritual legacy to your child and help him or her grow in faith. For most parents, helping our children grow spiritually doesn't come easily during the teenage years. Just as many young people enter adolescence, they begin to rebel a bit from their parents' faith. In the long run, this can be a great thing because it usually leads to a sense of ownership of their faith.

Many of you either did not have much of a spiritual legacy passed on to you from your parents or you have negative memories of childhood. If this is your situation, then you can be the transitional generation. On the other hand, if you come from a positive spiritual heritage, then passing the torch probably comes more easily for you. But for all of us, leaving a spiritual legacy for our children will take work and commitment.

Share your answer to one of the following questions with your group:

• What is a special family tradition that you remember from your childhood?

• What is a special family tradition that you enjoy celebrating with your own child?

keeping up with the Joneses

Watch this video segment about the Joneses' family traditions, and then answer the following question with your group:

• *The game-night tradition was a central part of Bud and Susie's lives. What types of spiritual traditions do you have in your family?*

One of the central themes of the Bible is that we are called to pass on our faith to the next generation. Every day in a practicing Jewish Orthodox home, the "Shema" is recited.[1] Part of this beautiful prayer reads, "Hear, O Israel: The Lord our God, the Lord is one. Love the Lord your God with all your heart and with all your soul and with all your strength. These commandments that I give you today are to be upon your hearts. Impress them on your children. Talk about them when you sit at home and when you walk along the road, when you lie down and when you get up. Tie them as symbols on your hands and bind them on your foreheads. Write them on the doorframes of your houses and on your gates" (Deuteronomy 6:4-9).

How can you "impress" your faith upon your child's heart? In order to help our children grow spiritually, it is important to get in touch with our own spiritual pilgrimage.

• What was one of your first "spiritual memories" as a child?

• Did your family have any spiritual traditions that were especially meaningful to you? any that were especially negative?

• What do you wish you could have received more of from your family while you were growing up?

Watch this video segment *from Jim Burns, and consider how it applies to your family's life.*

Notes:

For EXTRA Impact

Spend a few moments with your spouse or one other parent, and brainstorm some creative ways to start a new spiritual tradition in your home. One idea is to have your family invite your pastor's family to come over for dinner or to join you on a special outing. Prepare ahead of time any questions you might have for your pastor and your pastor's family. Create an environment in which your child can get to know the pastor as a "real person." Make it a fun and informative meeting that will give your child a chance to feel comfortable with your pastor. Another idea is to invite an elderly member of your church family over for dinner and ask him or her questions about his or her own faith journey. You could also discuss and pick out a secret gift of appreciation for your pastor or another member of the church family and deliver it anonymously.

• What is a new spiritual tradition you'd like to start in your family?

_____

_____

Going Deeper

SPIRITUAL DEVELOPMENT AND OUR CHILDREN'S FAITH

We live in an instant society in which we tend to think that we can all just instantly become spiritually mature. Often, our children make commitments to Christ—perhaps they go through confirmation classes or are baptized—and then, unfortunately, we expect them to instantly grow spiritually on their own. It is very important for us as parents to understand that faith develops in stages. Sanctification is a lifelong process. Our goals as parents are to help our children *own* their faith and to enable them to grow in Christian maturity.

There is more and more literature today that addresses the issue of faith development. One classic work on this subject is James Fowler's *Stages of Faith.*[2] Fowler identifies six stages: Intuitive-Projective, Mythic-Literal, Synthetic-Conventional, Individuative-Reflective, Conjunctive, and Universalizing. What do these stages look like in the life of a Christian teenager? Below you'll find my own definitions of what faith stages look like, based on the stages Fowler identified. Although these stages may typically move along age boundaries in Christian homes, that is not always the case because of differences between families, positive or negative faith decisions, or lack of spiritual knowledge.

STAGES OF FAITH

Stage 1: Intuitive-Projective. At this stage, a person has simply taken on his or her parents' faith.

Stage 2: Mythic-Literal. This stage is when a person moves from having only his or her parents' faith to having the faith of his or her extended family and perhaps his or her church.

Stage 3: Synthetic-Conventional. This is still an "unowned faith." During this stage, a person takes on the identity of his or her church or denomination. He or she still has not personalized his or her faith. This is often the stage of students entering junior high.

Stage 4: Individuative-Reflective. A person's faith is now his or her own. He or she has moved outside the bounds of relying on the faith of his or her significant others. This is usually a simplistic yet serious commitment.

Stage 5: Conjunctive. This stage is when a person's faith becomes more complex; he or she is reflective and aware of paradoxes and challenges to his or her beliefs. At this stage, one's faith does not shatter when one faces tough questions, such as suffering and evil in the world or unanswered prayer. There is a consistent commitment.

Stage 6: Universalizing. This is the most fully developed stage. A person has developed a world vision. He or she has a mission in life. His or her life, faith, and call from God make sense.

1. What stage of faith were you in as a teenager? Describe how and when your faith began to grow to the stage you are in now.

2. What stage or category of faith development would you say your teenager is in? Explain.

3. With this stage in mind, what do you think needs to take place for your child to grow spiritually?

4. How can a better understanding of the stages of faith development help you in leaving a spiritual legacy with your child?

In the Word

THE CALL FROM GOD

5. Read Deuteronomy 6:4-9. Summarize this biblical mandate in your own words.

6. How can we as parents place God's words "upon our hearts"?

7. What is the best way we can "impress them on your children"?

TALK ABOUT THE FAITH WITH YOUR CHILDREN

8. Reread Deuteronomy 6:7-8. In the Orthodox Jewish tradition, the people of faith literally tie Scripture (known as phylacteries) around their left arms, and they wear the Scripture on their foreheads.[3] This is a reminder that the Word of God should be with us while we work (our hands) and as we think (our heads). How can we, in the 21st century, accomplish this challenge of Scripture? What action steps can you take to honor this Scripture in the life of your family?

9. When is the last time you spoke candidly about your faith with your child? What *would* you like to share with your teenager about your own faith?

BUILD A FAMILY SPIRITUAL LEGACY

10. Reread Deuteronomy 6:9. What is the main point of this verse? What could it mean to write the Word on our doorframes and gates in modern times?

Many people allow circumstance and chance to build a spiritual legacy into the lives of their children. Yet, to really be successful, we as parents need a strategy to accomplish this most important biblical mandate.

Spiritual Legacy Strategy

- What are we presently doing in our home to pass on a spiritual legacy?

- What areas might need improvement?

- How would you describe your teenager's spiritual interest level or stage of faith? What can you do to meet your teenager where he or she is spiritually?

- What is your spiritual "dream" for your teenager? How would you like to see him or her grow?

- What are some steps you can take to leave a spiritual legacy in your child's life?

11. Read Proverbs 22:6. How is this promise a helpful reminder of God's presence in our parenting efforts?

So What?

Write the names of your child or children on an index card. Then use an ink pad to make a thumbprint on the card, directly on top of each of your children's names.

12. Discuss how the thumbprint symbolizes the impression you are making on your kids' lives.

- *What type of impression have you made so far?*

- *What type of impression do you want to leave?*

13. As a group, discuss ways to encourage, mentor, and disciple your children in their faith.

Here are some areas of discipleship that may be of importance to you:

- worship;
- one-on-one personally tailored discipleship;

- family devotions;
- praying together;
- serving together; and
- giving of your time, talents, and money together as a family.

Can you add any to this list?

_____

_____

_____

ACTION STEP

- What is one specific step you can take to help your teenager grow spiritually?

TALK About It

Talk about your own faith development with your teenager, and be willing to speak openly about your own struggles along the way. Being honest about challenges and tough questions will encourage your teenager as he or she faces similar issues.

Set aside thirty minutes this week to do this devotion as a family.

CREATE A FAMILY WORSHIP EXPERIENCE TOGETHER

In Old Testament times, much of the traditional teaching and celebrations were done in the home. One example of this is the Passover dinner, a tradition in which every child has a special part in the celebration. Unfortunately, the Christian church has moved away from worship in the home. We often rely solely on church services to meet our worship needs.

Work together to create a "worship service" for your family to do together at home. Brainstorm which elements of a family worship time you will include. (Some ideas are prayer, Scripture reading, sharing, songs, drama, or reading an inspirational story.) Then give each participating family member a part of the service, and go for it. Keep it short and to the point. Don't expect every portion of the service to go flawlessly. Just enjoy worshipping together!

Here's a simple format from the Burns' family Thanksgiving service:

1. Opening prayer (Christy)

2. Sharing of Scriptures

   • *Psalm 100 (Heidi)*

- *1 Thessalonians 5:18 (Rebecca)*
- *Psalm 136 (Christy)*
- *Psalm 34:1-4 (Mom)*
- *Philippians 4:6-7 (Dad)*

3. Communion (Dad)

4. Sharing of thankfulness (anyone who wants to share)

- *Our faith*
- *Our family*
- *Our friends*
- *Our food*

5. Discussion of how we as a family can serve God and serve others with our time, talents, and treasure. Action steps for the Advent season.

6. Singing of the "Lord's Prayer" (Christy)

Extra Impact @ HOME

Sponsor a Compassion child as a family!

Your family may want to consider sponsoring a Compassion child as a family ministry experience. Our family prays for our two Compassion children, gives money, writes to them, and feels like they are an important part of our lives. If you do sponsor a child, make sure that you take the time for the family to build a relationship with the child and not make it just another check to send to help a needy child.

For more info:
Compassion International
Colorado Springs, CO 80997
(800) 336-7676
www.compassion.com

participant guide endnotes

Session 1—Attitude Is Everything

1. Anthony E. Wolf, Ph.D., *Get Out of My Life, But First Could You Drive Me and Cheryl to the Mall?: A Parent's Guide to the New Teenager* (New York, NY: Farrar, Straus & Giroux, Inc., 1991).

2. David Elkind, *All Grown Up and No Place to Go: Teenagers in Crisis* (New York, NY: Perseus Books Group, 1998).

Session 5—Developing Media Discernment

1. Jolene L. Roehlkepartain, *Parents of Teenagers*, "The Lure of MTV," December 91/January 92.

2. Excerpted from "What You Need to Know About Television Violence," Youth Culture @ 2000 newsletter. Copyright © 1998 Center for Parent/Youth Understanding. Used by permission of the publisher. www.youthbuilders.com

3. Ibid.

4. Ibid.

5. Stephen Arterburn and Jim Burns, *Parents Guide to Top 10 Dangers Teens Face* (Wheaton, IL: Tyndale House Publishers, 1995), 69.

6. "What You Need to Know About Television Violence."

7. Ibid.

Session 6—Helping Your Teenager Grow Spiritually

1. *The NIV Study Bible* (Grand Rapids, MI: Zondervan Publishing House, 1985), 254.

2. James W. Fowler, *Stages of Faith: The Psychology of Human Development and the Quest for Meaning* (New York, NY: HarperCollins Publishers, 1981), 122-199.

3. *The NIV Study Bible*, 254.